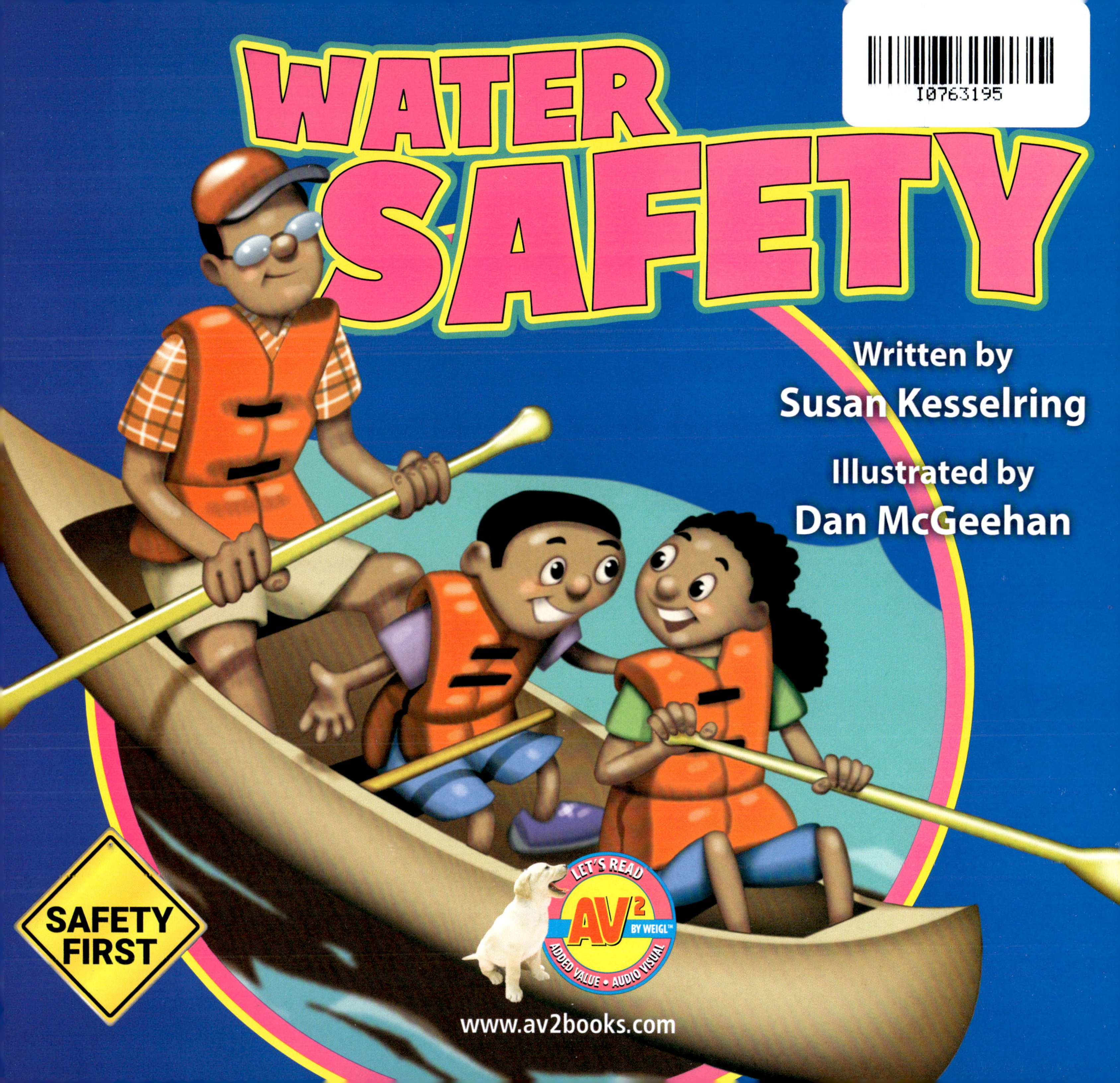
WATER SAFETY
Written by
Susan Kesselring
Illustrated by
Dan McGeehan
I0763195
SAFETY FIRST
LET'S READ
AV2
BY WEIGL
ADDED VALUE • AUDIO VISUAL
www.av2books.com

Go to www.av2books.com, and enter this book's unique code.

BOOK CODE

AVY29387

AV^2 by Weigl brings you media enhanced books that support active learning.

AV^2 provides enriched content that supplements and complements this book. Weigl's AV^2 books strive to create inspired learning and engage young minds in a total learning experience.

Your AV^2 Media Enhanced books come alive with...

Audio
Listen to sections of the book read aloud.

Video
Watch informative video clips.

Embedded Weblinks
Gain additional information for research.

Try This!
Complete activities and hands-on experiments.

Key Words
Study vocabulary, and complete a matching word activity.

Quizzes
Test your knowledge.

Slide Show
View images and captions, and prepare a presentation.

... and much, much more!

Published by AV^2 by Weigl
350 5th Avenue, 59th Floor New York, NY 10118
Website: www.av2books.com

Library of Congress Cataloging-in-Publication Data

Names: Kesselring, Susan, author.
Title: Water safety / Susan Kesselring.
Description: New York, NY : AV^2 by Weigl, 2020. | Series: Safety first | Audience: K to Grade 3.
Identifiers: LCCN 2018053409 (print) | LCCN 2018054617 (ebook) | ISBN 9781489699565 (Multi User Ebook) | ISBN 9781489699589 (Single User Ebook) | ISBN 9781489699558 (hardcover : alk. paper) | ISBN 9781489699572 (softcover : alk. paper)
Subjects: LCSH: Swimming--Safety measures--Juvenile literature. | Aquatic sports--Safety measures--Juvenile literature.
Classification: LCC GV838.53.S24 (ebook) | LCC GV838.53.S24 K468 2020 (print) | DDC 797.2/1083--dc23
LC record available at https://lccn.loc.gov/2018053409

Printed in the United States of America in Brainerd, Minnesota
1 2 3 4 5 6 7 8 9 0 22 21 20 19 18

112018
102918

Project Coordinator: Jared Siemens Designer: Ana María Vidal

First published by The Child's World in 2011

WATER SAFETY

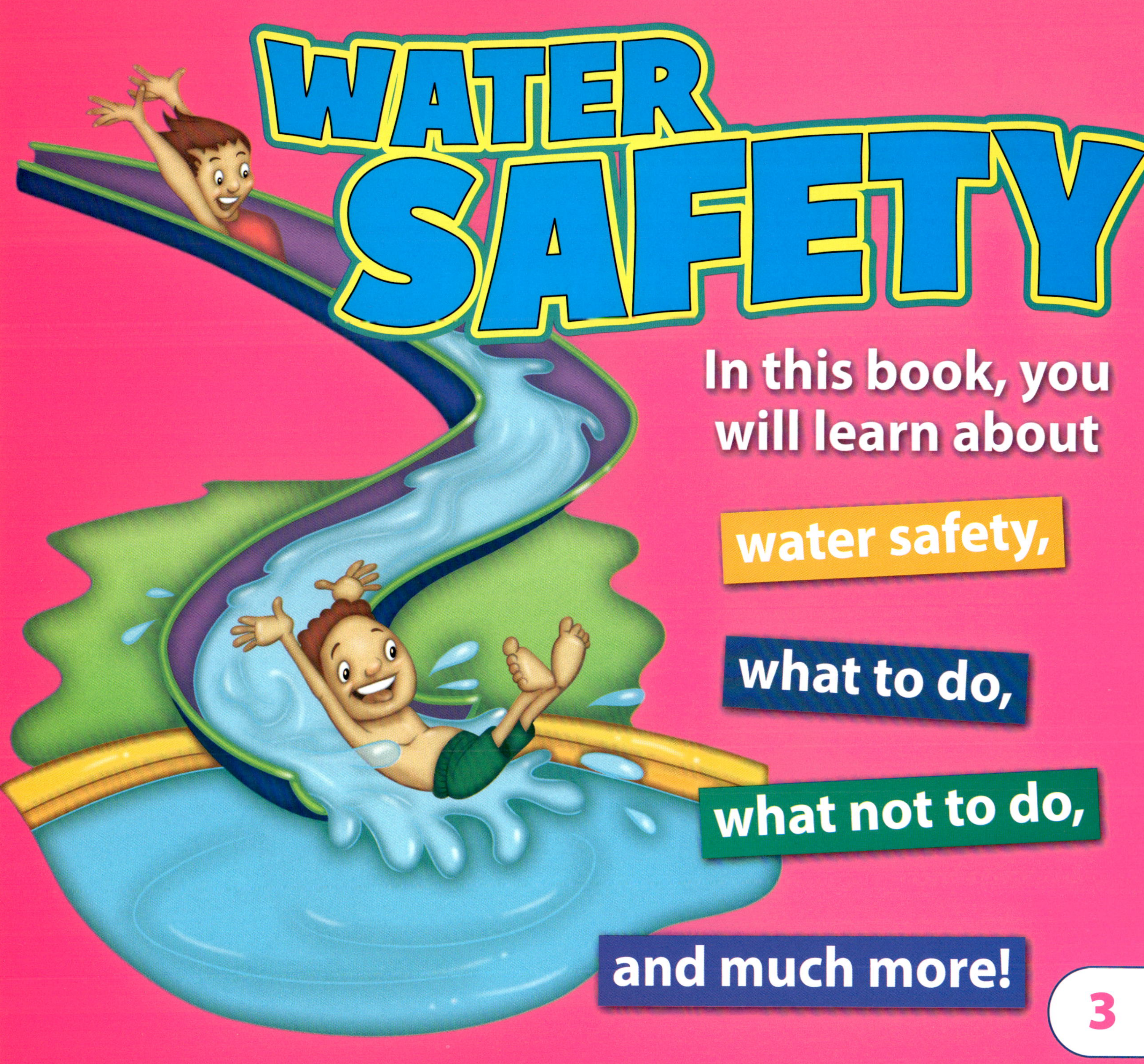

In this book, you will learn about

water safety,

what to do,

what not to do,

and much more!

What is your favorite way to splash? Are you a diver or a water slider? Do you like to ride the ocean's waves? Can you touch the bottom of the pool with your belly? Do you race your canoe across a pond?

Playing around water is a blast! If you follow a few safety rules, you can have tons of fun and still be safe.

What's the best way to stay safe around water? Learn to swim! Don't worry if you are not a strong swimmer yet. Ask an adult to teach you how.

Maybe your parents will bring you to swimming lessons. Once you know how to swim, you can play in the deep end.

Practice your swimming by holding on to the side of the pool. Then, float on your belly and kick your legs.

Is a pool your favorite place to swim? Ask your parents how deep you can go. Remember to always have a parent or lifeguard watching.

Swim with a friend. It's more fun! Plus, you can look out for each other. The pool deck can be slippery. Be sure not to run!

There are many kinds of pools. Some sit on top of the ground. Others are in the ground.

Always wear sunscreen when swimming outdoors. Put more sunscreen on after you have been in the water.
9FT
9FT

You can't wait to get in the water! Just don't dive headfirst if the water is shallow. You could get seriously hurt. Jump in feet first, and look before you jump. You don't want to land on top of someone.

If you want to dive, ask an adult where it is safe to do so. The water should be at least 9 feet (2.7 meters) deep.

In pools and hot tubs, stay away from the drains on the bottom. Keep food and gum out of your mouth while you are in the water.

The water in hot tubs can be very hot. Have an adult check the temperature and join you in the water. Hot tub uses should be no more than 20 minutes long.

Playing at a water park is a whole day's worth of fun! Wear a life jacket if you are not a strong swimmer. Always walk to each ride.

Check the rules before you try each slide. Go down each slide feet first. Make sure a parent or lifeguard is close by, just in case.

Water parks are busy places. What should you do if you lose your parents? Go to one of the workers at the water park and ask for help.

Swimming in a lake or a river can be tricky. You can't always tell how deep the water is. There could be sharp rocks on the bottom. Wear water shoes to protect your feet.

Stay away from very weedy spots that might trap your legs and arms. Always swim with an adult.

To build your own sand castle, you need wet sand and a small shovel. Building it close to the water is a good idea.

Oceans have strong waves and currents. These can be strong enough to pull you out into deep water. Have your parents check when the currents are too strong to swim.

To stay safe, swim where a lifeguard is watching you. Face the waves so you can see them coming. Always swim with a buddy. If you see jellyfish, stay away. They can sting!

How fast can you paddle a canoe? Have you ever ridden in a kayak or a motorboat? It's so much fun to zip over the water.

Whenever you are on a boat, wear a life jacket that is snug on your body. If you fall in, you'll float! Stay sitting while your boat is gliding along so you don't tip.

Now you know how to be safe in pools, hot tubs, water parks, rivers, lakes, and oceans.

Here is one last tip for any kind of water play. Do you hear thunder rumbling? Is a storm on its way? Get out of the water right away! If you are boating, get to shore quickly. Take shelter in a car or a building.

Lightning is electricity. Electricity travels easily through water. If you are in water when lightning strikes, you could be shocked.

KEY WORDS

Research has shown that as much as 65 percent of all written material published in English is made up of 300 words. These 300 words cannot be taught using pictures or learned by sounding them out. They must be recognized by sight. This book contains 123 common sight words to help young readers improve their reading fluency and comprehension. This book also teaches young readers several important content words, such as proper nouns.

Page	Sight Words First Appearance
4	a, are, can, do, is, like, of, or, the, to, water, way, what, with, you, your
5	and, around, be, few, follow, for, have, how, I, if, me, still, tell, watch, will
7	an, ask, by, don't, end, know, learn, not, on, once, play, side, then
9	always, each, go, in, it's, kinds, look, many, more, other, out, place, run, some, there
10	after, been, put, when
11	at, before, could, feet, first, get, it, just, land, should, so, want, where
13	away, food, from, keep, long, no, than, uses, very, while
15	close, down, help, life, make, one, try, walk
17	might, river, that
18	good, idea, need, own, small
19	enough, face, into, see, them, these, they, too
21	along, much, over
23	any, car, hear, here, its, last, now, right, take, through

Page	Content Words First Appearance
4	belly, bottom, canoe, diver, ocean, pond, pool, slider, waves
5	fun, safety rules
7	adult, legs, lessons, parents, swimmer
9	friend, ground, lifeguard, pool deck
10	outdoors, sunscreen
13	drains, gum, hot tubs, minutes, mouth, temperature
15	life jacket, ride, slide, water park, workers
17	arms, lake, rocks, spots, water shoes
18	castle, sand, shovel
19	buddy, currents, jellyfish
21	boat, body, kayak, motorboat
23	building, electricity, lightning, shelter, shore, storm, thunder

Check out www.av2books.com for activities, videos, audio clips, and more!

 **Go to www.av2books.com.**

 **Enter book code.** AVY29387

 **Fuel your imagination online!**

www.av2books.com